For
Cecily Forwell

Enjoy !

FROM HUMBLE BEGINNINGS: TALES OF A NATIVE SON

BY WILLIAM FRANKLIN ANDREWS

ILLUSTRATED BY HANNAH MURIEL ANDREWS

CHRONIC DISCONTENT BOOKS
FRANKLIN, TENNESSEE

TALES OF A NATIVE SON

Published December 2017 by Chronic Discontent Books
Thomas Brent Andrews, Publisher
Franklin, Tennessee

ISBN 978-0-9767056-4-2

Illustrated by Hannah Muriel Andrews

Cover design and production by Jeff Hottle

Contents designed by Ginny Andrews

Cover and chapter heading art by Hannah Muriel Andrews

The Chronic Discontent Books logo is borrowed from *Ancient Sichuan and the Unification of China*, by Steven F. Sage, State University of New York Press, 1992. The bone inscription is believed to be approximately 3,200 years old. Writes Sage: "Conjecture relates this eye to a legendary version of Shu origins, mentioning a 'vertical-eyed man' (*zong mu zhi ren*), figuratively perhaps meaning a 'man of vision.'"

ACKNOWLEDGEMENTS

This book would not have been possible without others who listened to the stories I told about my life. Thanks to my son Brent Andrews – my editor, publisher and constant friend who guided this project from the beginning; to my beloved wife, Carolyn, who listened with patience as I told and retold the stories with some embellishment each time; to my granddaughter Hannah Andrews who won all of our hearts with her perfect portrayal in pictures; to my daughter Becky Steere and to my long-time office manager Toni Ruiz for thoughtful proofreading of the manuscript; to my daughter-in-law Ginny Andrews for crafting the interior layout; and to Jeff Hottle for the cover design.

CONTENTS

Prologue

'Traveling Light'

I am a stranger traveling light.
You see no heavy load I bring;
I'm on the road both day and night,
And as I go along my songs I sing.

There are no lines drawn on a map;
So I must struggle on and make my way.
Though along the way I hear the taps,
Of feet left here from yesterday.

Now I must make a mark my own;
A line drawn on a map that's true,
So just in case you're lost in fear,
I'll leave a light along the way for you.

How A Country Boy Makes A Buck

Franklin in the late 1940s and early 1950s was a small country town. If you wanted fried chicken you either raised your own or purchased it from one of the many small grocery stores that were operating in Franklin at the time. The H.G. Hill grocery store was on the southwest corner of Fourth Avenue South and Main Street, and just down a couple of stores Mr. Ed Thurman had a grocery that was called Thurman's Market. Mr. Thurman had a complete line of groceries and always had a great display of fresh fruits and vegetables neatly stacked on the street in front of the store.

Inside Thurman's Market were many shelves with a wide variety of canned goods and boxes of Quaker and Crystal Wedding Oats along with other items his customers needed.

The meat department was run by a couple of local men, one of whom was my uncle who had recently returned from serving in the U.S. Army. He needed someone to kill the chickens that were brought to the rear of the store by local farmers and kept in coops until they were ready for someone's table. I along with another uncle quickly volunteered for the work. Well this job only lasted one day.

We hauled the chickens up the steps in the rear of the store to a large warehouse-type room that had all we needed to perform our work.

I was a tough farm boy, undaunted by any job that required stamina and grit, but I was totally unprepared for killing chickens over the store at Thurman's Market.

The squawking made by these poor creatures facing death and a scalding bath along with the horrible odor was more than enough to make me leave my new job and head back to the farm.

My uncle continued to work at Thurman's for a while and a story from his days as a butcher there has been handed down to me.

It seems that a lady appeared at the meat department counter one day and asked for about a two-pound frying chicken. Well there was only one chicken in the rear cooler and it only weighed one-and-a-half pounds. That problem was quickly remedied by the placement of a thumb on the scale, bringing the chicken's weight to exactly two pounds. Well lo and behold the lady changed her mind and stated that maybe she only needed a chicken that weighed about one-and-a-half pounds. So my uncle returned to the cooler and brought forth the same chicken that really weighed that amount. The lady's next statement caused our veteran soldier to do some really quick thinking when she stated, "You know, maybe I'll just take both of them."

As cool as a soldier in the heat of battle my uncle replied, "I am sorry, ma'am, but I have promised that chicken to another customer."

A few years later a large chicken processing plant was constructed on Second Avenue South at South Margin Street where the antique mall is presently located. That uncle became the manager of the Dixie Poultry processing plant.

The Easter-Egg Hunt

The Easter season of 1946 found me in first grade at Franklin Elementary School. At the time I was living about two-and-a-half miles from the school, which was located at Five Points where the Williamson County Archives Museum is today.

My teacher was Miss M- C- B-. Her name must remain secret as it is very prominent in the Franklin area today. Anyhow as the Easter season approached it was announced that we would be going to the Andrews Farm with our classmates for an Easter egg hunt. The Andrewses of that farm were no relation to me.

The teacher told all of the students in the class to bring a dozen hard-boiled eggs to school the next day for the trip. We would paint them at school and take them to the farm for our hunt.

Well I might as well have asked for a side of beef as to ask for eggs. In those days eggs at sixty cents per dozen were a cash crop that my grandmother used to help manage the family budget. When I arrived at home that evening I did not bring up the subject that I was in need of a dozen eggs. I would just not have eggs for the hunt.

Upon my arrival at school the next day my teacher asked, "Frank, did you bring a dozen eggs?"

"I could not bring any eggs as we did not have any to spare," I replied.

"That's all right, Frank," she said. "You will go to the Andrews Farm with us but you will not be participating in the egg hunt."

Every time I pass the old house on Lewisburg Pike I can still see a small boy sitting on the steps as the other children joyfully hunted for hidden eggs.

I remember my sad feelings when the other children would approach me with the question, "Frank, why are you not hunting eggs?"

'Take This Job And Shove It'

It was a hot April day, about 1967. The Ford glass plant was already heating up for the day.

Early in my shift as foreman in the windshield-finishing department my general foreman showed up with an urgent need for a particular type of windshield. His instructions to me were: "You will get 2,900 pieces in the box for shipping today, or your job will be in jeopardy. They are holding the line at the assembly plant in Dearborn, Michigan for this part."

"Well, sir," I answered back, "could you just do me one favor before you leave?"

"Of course I will," he said. "And what would that be?"

"Just give me five minutes with the authority to hire or fire some of these careless workers and I will guarantee production," I said.

"Well," he said, "as you know with the power of the United Auto Workers Union I cannot do that. I am sorry but I wish I could."

In the late sixties the union had gained such a stranglehold on the auto manufacturing companies that it was almost impossible to fire an employee. If you had asked for a little extra effort the first reply would have been, "Please call me a committeeman!"

Well I promised the boss that I would do my best and I turned to the two workers packing that windshield and asked as kindly as I knew how for a good day's work.

However, they were not in the mood to make production that day. So they slow-walked all day and managed to pack about one-half the normal production. Near the end of the shift I walked up to them and thanked them for a good day's work.

With wry smiles they both reared back as one stated, "It sure was a long, hot day and we gave you our very best."

In my frustration I made them a promise: They would never see me in that hot old plant again.

From there I dropped by to see my boss in his office and made the same promise to him.

I walked out of the plant that day and never looked back. I was finally free to explore other opportunities. Now here it is almost fifty years later and I have never regretted telling my boss to "take this job and shove it."

No Lies Allowed

In this story a small country boy gets a whipping for lying – and the boy is me!

Grandma was a very religious woman, not tolerant of liars. I knew how she felt about lying when she came to me to ask about the salve bottle someone had discovered on the pathway out back.

It had been broken by someone using it as a target! And that someone had hit the bulls-eye! The bottle of salve lay shattered on the path.

Salve was a very necessary medicine for a poor farm family with little money to buy a replacement. It had been purchased from the J.R. Watkins traveling salesman who came to the farm on his route serving the rural community of sharecroppers and other farm families living in Williamson County, Tennessee in the mid-1940s.

Well as it turned out I happened to be the last one seen with the bottle, so I must be the guilty one! If only I would admit it, I would be spared the switch. However I could not admit doing something that I had not done. I did not break the bottle of salve! I would not admit to a "crime" that I did not commit.

Some other person in our large family was guilty. The blame was being placed on me, the young and innocent one. Well the switching began with a promise from Grandma: "If you will just admit that you broke the medicine bottle I will stop the whipping!" Still I would not lie on myself. The whipping continued until I realized that it was not going to stop until I told a lie and confessed!

Grandma hugged me and cried along with me as she told me the eternal punishment for lying. I carried the lying guilt for many years.

One day many years later an uncle had a conscience breakdown and told the truth. He had been the guilty one and was sorry after all these years that he had let little Frank take such a whipping.

I guess you probably know the rest of the story. Grandma gave this adult, married son of hers a real flogging that he will probably never forget!

Late but welcome apologies were given to me. Now I am free from the lie that I told to stop the whipping.

Death Of A Hundred-Dollar Car

"Never go into debt unless it is a real emergency."

These words were sage advice I had received growing up with my grandparents on the farm. I was thinking this when I approached Mr. Fuller Arnold at Williamson County Bank about a loan to purchase a car.

The year was 1954 and I needed a car for traveling back and forth to school and my job at a local auto repair shop. In order to purchase this 1948 Ford 2-Door Coupe I needed to borrow the total price – 110 dollars.

Mr. Arnold made the loan. I purchased the car and my payments were ten dollars a month. This was quite a sum for my budget, but I reckoned that I could make it since my salary at the shop was fifteen dollars a week.

The car was quite a beauty – a two-toned blue-and-white coupe that had been painted with house-paint and a brush. The interior had been restyled and the steering wheel had a cool leather cover along with a turning-knob. The six-cylinder engine ran smoothly and the transmission was a stick-shift in the floor that I had learned to operate in my experience driving the old farm truck.

I would usually drive my car until I ran out of gas. I would park it at that point and walk home or to school or work.

Those idyllic days of the fifties found the price of gas at twenty-one cents a gallon. Postage was three cents and steak was sixty-nine cents per pound. I could not afford steak and I had no use for mailing letters. However, the price of gas caused me some concern because at twenty-one cents a gallon I could soon be burning up two or three dollars a week.

My first car became very dear to me and after graduating from Franklin High School in 1957, I passed it on to a younger aunt who was still in school.

As the years have gone by I have been privileged to own many fine cars. In fact there was a year when I traded cars three times before I got the one I really wanted. I would trade any of those modern cars today for that sweet little Ford Coupe.

My little two-toned Ford met an awful fate. It seems Grandpa decided his young daughter was driving too much and needed to be taught a lesson. Unbeknownst to my aunt, he chained my car to a large cedar tree.

One day my aunt decided to go to town. Not knowing about the chain, she cranked the car up and took off!

She left the entire rear-end of my car chained to that cedar tree. The car was disabled forever.

That must have been a painful death for a hundred-dollar car.

Spotlight On Spook Stories

The winter of 1948 found me living in a sharecropper shack on a farm where the Royal Oaks residential development is now located. The farm was a productive agricultural estate.

Our family tended the entire farm containing about two hundred acres. We were the last generation of mule farmers and our mule teams could be seen daily plowing the straight rows of corn and tobacco that were the chief crops.

Our home on the farm was two sharecropper shacks.

A sharecropper shack was not a luxury home. It was only basic shelter from the rain and cold. It was constructed of oak and pine planks with a tin roof and no insulation, no screens, no electricity or running water. Often we found chicken-snakes on the porch or falling from the attic. The holes in the floor allowed the opportunity to feed the chickens without going outside. Our drinking water came from a spring out front and our toilet facility was a two-hole outhouse situated far enough away from the house to give a boy good exercise on his daily trip.

Our family was large and one sharecropper shack was not sufficient to house us all. Grandma and Grandpa lived in what we called the "lower house" with the smaller children. This shack had three rooms. The living room had a wood stove and double bed. The bedroom had two double beds with straw mattresses where four or five children slept cross-wise on each bed. We had no need for closets as we just took off our clothes and hung them on a nail until we could put them back on the next morning. If your clothes became soiled before wash day that was just tough. You wore them to school dirty.

Our older boys lived in a smaller shack about a quarter-mile up the creek. I would often make my way up to their house and spend hours with them until it was time for bed.

One winter night with a good amount of snow on the ground I decided I would visit the older boys. I had an old flashlight that would barely shine because the batteries had almost expired. I carried it along the path and across the foot-log that crossed the creek along the way.

As I approached the older boys' small shack I noticed that there was very little light coming from the windows. I crept up to the rear window and heard ghost stories being told. I listened intently for a few minutes and then raised the old flashlight up to the window and shined it through the glass.

What chaos I suddenly created! Yelling and diving to the floor were six or eight frightened, half-grown boys scattering as quickly as possible. They all thought a ghost had really appeared!

I did not have a peaceful reunion with that group of scared young men that night. I remember a thrashing at their hands and although not damaged physically, I made a fast trip back down the hill.

When I reached home Grandma was waiting to help salve my wounded pride. I learned my lesson and never made another surprise visit to the upper house.

Did You Say 'Whisk Broom' Or 'Rest Room'?

The day started off as usual at the local Gulf Service Station where I was working. It was the summer of 1956 and I was employed as summer help. The station was located at the Harpeth River bridge on East Main Street in Franklin. This is where the Boat House Restaurant is now. My two uncles who owned the station took great pride in keeping it clean and attractive for the many customers the station served in those days.

My duties included filling cars with gas as they arrived, sweeping out the car, washing the windshield, checking the oil and other things such as cleaning the rest rooms. In those days in Franklin the gasoline filling stations still gave real service to their customers. Gas was about twenty cents per gallon and

every car needed an oil change after one thousand miles.

It must have been the hottest day of summer when a lady pulled into the station and began speaking a strange, Yankee English. As she rolled up I bounded to the bay area ready to serve her.

She rolled her window down and accepted my good morning asking a question in her strange tongue: "Do you have a rest room?"

Due to the unfamiliar accent I thought she said "whisk broom."

Being the helpful and courteous attendant that I was, I simply replied, "No, ma'am, but if you will back up to the air hose over there I will blow it out for you."

Well you can guess what happened: Fast as lightning the young lady closed her window and burned the rubber on her tires speeding away.

I headed back into the station where I was met by a concerned uncle who demanded to know what had just happened.

I told my uncle what had taken place and stated that I was at a loss as to why the lady had left in such a hurry.

"Well, son," he replied, "she did not say 'whisk broom.' She must have said 'rest room.'"

I was immediately relieved of my front-of-the-station customer-greeting job. Until my employment ended late that summer I was relegated to a lowly job as grease monkey. Most of all there would be no public face for me.

I frequently dine at the Boat House Restaurant today. I am amazed at the number of Yankees I meet. It sure is a good thing that long ago I learned to understand their "foreign" language!

It's So Easy To Write A Song

It was a normal midnight shift in the late sixties at the Ford glass plant in West Nashville where I was employed as an inspector.

The assembly line was running full-speed as the windshields passed through my inspection booth. The finished windshields were on their way to workers down the line who would place them in packing crates for shipment to assembly plants around the world. Once there, they would be placed into automobiles.

My fellow workers and I took great pride in inspecting the glass for any defects that would alter a car buyer's vision while driving the final product.

As I was busy with my work a co-worker walked up

for conversation. He began telling me a story of a country song that he had written. It was a nice country tune he had titled "Write Me A Picture Of Our Love." He had just had his song recorded by George Hamilton IV and was anticipating great success and a new career.

Well you see I had been writing for a long time myself, but had never had any success in getting anything that I had written published or even listened to by anyone. So with a little bit of disdain in my voice I said to my friend, "Shucks, Vance, anybody can write a song!"

To my surprise he said, "Why don't you write one?"

Caught off-guard I said, "Give me a ten minute break from this line and I will write you a song."

He immediately took the marking chalk from my hand and said, "Buddy you are on."

In shock I took a seat on a packing crate about twenty feet away. I picked up a scrap of paper and prayed, "Lord, I have made a fool of myself, could you rescue me?"

The words immediately came into my head and I began
to write.

"Roll Wagon Wheel Roll"

I left St. Joe a happy young man;
I had a great future, I had lots of plans.
But life on the trail was heartache and fear;
These injuns and deserts have caused many tears.

Mary told me when I left St. Joe,
"Go make your fortune; go find the gold.
"Then hurry back home and soon we'll be wed."
Now the telegraph tells me that Mary is dead.

Roll, roll, wagon wheel roll.
Roll, wagon wheel roll.
My heart is bitter; my body is cold.
Roll, wagon wheel roll.

Well I've made my fortune; I found the gold.
But life has no meaning since Mary is gone.
Forever I'll wander these prairies so cold.
Roll, roll, wagon wheel roll.

Roll, roll, wagon wheel roll.
Roll, wagon wheel roll.
My heart is bitter; my body is cold.
Roll, wagon wheel roll.

I made the deadline of ten minutes with a little to spare, and returned to the inspection booth where my friend was anxiously waiting. I sang my new song to him as he stood in total disbelief.

"You could not have written that song!" he said.

"Well have you ever heard it?" I asked.

"No," he admitted, "but what you just did is impossible."

I did not tell him where the words really came from. Maybe I should have told him about the prayer I said as I sat down to write.

Maybe some day a country singer looking for a western trail song will find this one. I leave it as a gift to my son Brent who has encouraged me to tell the story.

Poor Boy Vs. Rich Man

Life on the farm in the early 1950s was often a challenge due to a lack of money.

In my first year at Franklin High School in 1953, I was living on a farm on Moran Road in the Grassland community. The school bus traveled a circuitous route from the high school to my house by first traveling north on Hillsboro Pike past Moran Road and entering Sneed Road. At that time Sneed was a narrow, one-lane gravel road. It was accessed from high on the hill north of where its junction with Hillsboro Pike is now. From there it made its way west through Sawyer's Bend and then to Moran Road.

Most days when the weather permitted I left the bus at Moran Road and walked the short distance across the river to our farm.

One spring day a wealthy lady from the neighborhood stopped to give me a lift. Before our trip was completed she had offered me a job working for her on Saturdays. Her offer was four dollars a day.

At the time this was good pay for a farm boy, and I accepted her offer and asked when I could start.

She replied, "Why don't you come around Saturday morning around seven?"

The job had been approved by my grandfather with the firm assurance that my usual chores would not go undone. So the following Saturday I got up early enough to complete all of my chores before heading off to work. It was still bright and early when I left our farm.

When I arrived at the lady's farm my first day was well-planned. My job for the day was to pluck all the dandelions in the lawn by the roots using a small forked tool and deliver them to a spot for disposal. There were thousands of these pesky flowers scattered around in the lush grass.

I worked diligently all day with only a little time out for my lunch. It consisted of two of Grandma's biscuits stuffed with bacon.

Four o'clock in the evening found me very tired but extremely happy as I headed home with money in my pocket. I would have enough to see the latest Western at the Franklin Theatre and sufficient money for the next week at school.

I was really looking forward to my next Saturday. I had schemed all week about how I was going to spend the money I would make. I showed up at the appointed time.

Well to my surprise I was met by the husband of this
wealthy woman. He was standing tall in the doorway. He
looked down on a poor, freckled, red-headed boy in
short britches. He was the king and I was his underling.

The king explained to me in no uncertain terms that four
dollars a day was not an acceptable price to pay for a
school boy with no other means for earning money. He
told me that I could continue working for him but the
pay would be two dollars a day.

I could have dropped off the earth from the anxiety that suddenly overwhelmed me. How must I respond? Two dollars was not very much but it was hard to turn down. After all I could just cut my budget in half and proceed with the work. But no, my response was, "Sir, I am a poor boy and I need the money but I do not have to slave for you to live. I think I will just go home."

I felt good about myself until I thought about what Grandpa would say about me quitting my job before the second day was completed. When I arrived at our farm I explained to Grandpa what had happened.

Grandpa replied, "Son you are exactly right in what you did. We may be poor but we do not have to kiss anyone's rear-end to make our living. We will be just fine without him."

Payback for this selfish neighbor came a few months later when I shot his mean old German shepherd dog.

One of my duties on the farm was tending the sheep and protecting them from dogs. Well early one morning I was awakened by a loud bleating sound and I knew immediately that the sheep were in danger.

I quickly arose and grabbed pants, shoes and shirt and a twelve-gauge shotgun that we had for hunting, and proceeded out to the sheep pasture.

A large black dog was chasing our sheep and they were in total distress. Lambs were being scattered from their mothers and this was creating a loud and frantic scene in the pasture.

I raised the gun and took aim, and without knowing whose dog was the culprit I let go with a loud blast and the vicious dog toppled over.

Now what? I soon realized that I had shot a neighbor's dog and that neighbor was my old wealthy ex-employer.

I knew what must be done. I must call this neighbor on the phone to explain what had happened. The phone conversation ended with a loud exclamation, "Son you had better hope that you have not killed my dog. My dog does not chase sheep."

He arrived in a mighty huff just a few minutes later and as he exited his truck he yelled, "You have not heard the last of this."

He moved over to his dog, picked him up and put him into his pickup truck. His threat did not frighten me in the least. After all what could he do to a poor moneyless farm boy who had just shot his dog?

Before he left he exclaimed, "Boy you are in serious trouble and you will be hearing from me soon."

I replied, "If your dog does not chase sheep there should not be any wool in his teeth." I quickly opened the dog's mouth and there was the evidence: His teeth were full of wool.

I never heard from the king again.

A Nickel Sack Of Country Gentleman Tobacco; Or, A Long Walk From McPherson's Store

Mr. McPherson had everything in his store at Forest Home. Customers could buy feed, seed, groceries and most anything needed for farming.

The small frame building was typical of the many general stores that were scattered around Williamson County in the 1950s. These stores were the social gathering places of their communities.

Here at the end of the day tired farmers sat on the bench outside, chewing tobacco and solving the world's problems. In the summer hard-fought elections were held here, and candidates worked the crowds frantically to secure votes.

The year was 1953 and life on the farm on Moran Road was hard. At the time we were tenant farmers on the historic Jim Robinson Farm. Money was scarce and little thought was given to wasting it on an unnecessary evil

39

like tobacco.

However, tonight was special and my friend and I decided to walk to the store about four miles from my house. We arrived at Mr. McPherson's store five or ten minutes before he closed for the night.

It did not take us long to spend our limited funds. My friend purchased a nickel sack of Country Gentleman tobacco, and I bought a penny stick of licorice. Country Gentleman was a small sack of smoking tobacco with yellow strings to tie up the opening at the top. Attached to the side of the sack were sufficient papers for rolling your cigarettes. I was not a smoker at this age but my friend was already addicted.

It was dark as we headed home. The road was narrow and encased by an overgrowth of trees in many areas. The Old Natchez Trace Road which led us back to the farm had many historic homes. One of the most prominent was Old Town. Old Town was near ancient Indian mounds that are still visible today. The Harpeth River ran near the roadway and there was an old stone bridge that Andrew Jackson crossed on his way to defeat the British at New Orleans.

As we approached the extremely dark area along the river we just knew that we could see ghosts in front of us.

The darkness was not the only problem we encountered. I was barefoot, and the rocks were causing considerable damage to my feet. My friend was wearing a pair of black combat boots that his uncle who had served in the Army in Korea had given him. He had worn the boots completely out and nails were piercing his heels as we walked home. Finally in his distress he removed the boots and we walked barefoot together.

Although we were completely spent we ran the last mile to the farm. The next time we visited McPherson's store we made sure that the night would not catch us on our way back home.

Escape From Miss Jones

Miss Jones was a fifth-grade teacher at Howard School in Nashville in the 1950s. I happened into her class by reason of leaving the farm and my loving grandparents to finish my life with my mother. Mother had recently married her fourth husband, and claimed to be ready to take back her two children whom she had abandoned a few years earlier. When school ended for the summer she took my sister Jean and me to the city to live with her.

Howard School was just across the street from our Second Avenue apartment. This made it very convenient for us to walk to school. Also on the school campus was the Children's Museum where I spent many happy hours that summer.

The Nashville Fire Department had a station two doors up the street from our house, and my friend Wayne who lived across the street and I had a lot of fun calling in a fire and watching the firemen scramble to get going. The real fun was when they returned and Wayne and I would show up at the fire hall and inquire as to where the fire was.

We always got the same answer from the captain: "One of these days young men you are going to jail for this!"

Soon school started and I found myself in Miss Jones' fifth-grade classroom. Miss Jones was the miserable part of my life in the city. I sometimes thought of her as the "teacher from Hell."

It seems to me that she took great pride in letting everyone know how ignorant this small country boy was. At this time I had not learned cursive so I just printed all my letters and connected them with a line either at the top or the bottom. I was most embarrassed the day she held my paper up to the class to show them "how well" I could write.

She told me in no uncertain terms, "The correct cursive form of all the letters in the alphabet is posted around this room. Young man, you will never turn in another paper with such disgraceful form."

I cried from fright as I explained to my mother my fears of this dreaded teacher. Mother had no means to solve my problem and it was obvious to me that she did not plan to intercede.

The following weekend was time for us to go back to the farm for a visit with my grandparents.

After being "home" for a short while I realized how much I missed living with Grandma. Everything about the country was wonderful and the city life was just not right for me. I humbly turned to my little grandmother.

"Grandma, may I come home?"

Being the kind and loving woman that she was Grandma replied simply.

"Son, you may come home any time but you are not going to be running back and forth."

"Grandma," I said, "if you will just let me come home I will never leave again."

Looking back Miss Jones may have been an angel sent from Heaven to save me, as opposed to the teacher from Hell. If she had been a little bit kind to me I might have stayed in Nashville and wound up in real trouble, just like the captain predicted.

How I Quit Smoking In 20 Years

"If I catch you smoking again I will kill you."

These are the words that I heard from my wife for the entire time that I was guilty of this awful sin. I became addicted to this weed during my Army days and for years against the wishes of my wife I was a slipper-smoker: That is, I slipped around to do my smoking. One time, sneaking a cigarette, I literally slipped and fell on a frozen patio and almost became a smoking casualty.

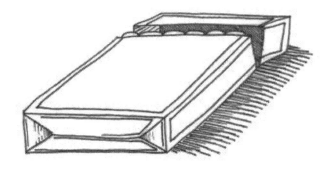

Quitting was easy. I quit more times than I can recall. Usually I quit when I had just bought a brand-new pack which I would throw away.

About twenty years ago I quit for good. My wife, Carolyn, and I were on our way to church when she accidentally dropped something on the car floor. As she reached to pick it up I reflexively moved my knee over in order to protect my cigarettes hidden under the floor mat.

"You have cigarettes hidden under that floor mat!" she charged. She thought I had whipped this awful habit.

"You will never know!" I replied angrily, knowing I was caught.

Gosh, did all hell break loose in that car on the way to church! The car was rocking back and forth as she fought for the floor mat and I fought for control of the car!

Upon arrival at church she exited the car and slammed the door so hard I fully expected the windows to explode. My dilemma was magnified by the fact that I was probably headed for Hell as well as a divorce.

My solution: I simply drove up about fifty feet and quit smoking again. I threw almost a brand-new pack into the shrubs by the church. This time I had help in quitting. As I threw the pack into the shrubs I called upon God to help me quit.

"Lord, I have quit this deadly habit many times before but I have found it impossible," I prayed earnestly. "Lord would you please take these cigarettes and this thing that is wrecking my soul and my home?"

It worked! HE answered. To this day I have had no desire to smoke – the desire that drove me to lie to my own wife, to slip out in the dark and nearly break my hip on the ice, to sin and harm myself.

I want to give full credit to my maker for saving my soul, and my marriage.

A Team Of Mules In Deep Water

The summer of 1954 was an eventful time in my life.

I had just finished my freshman year at Franklin High School and I was living on the Robinson Farm on Moran Road in the Grassland community of northern Williamson County.

The summer started off hot and dry and our small pond in the pasture lot went dry. In order to water our stock it was necessary to load up ten or twelve fifty-gallon barrels on our tired steel farm wagon, hitch up the mules, and trek across the road to a larger pond.

There, from a hundred-year-old pond with at least a foot of black mud on the bottom we would fill the barrels and travel back and empty them into our stock-tank. This task was repeated about three times a week.

This particular hot day I was accompanied by a young friend who was spending most of the summer at our house. The young friend lived with us and was a regular hand on the farm. Setting out, we could never have

50

guessed that today would bring an adventure of a lifetime, that tragedy would almost overtake us.

We did our usual hook-up of the mules and loaded the barrels onto the wagon. Upon arrival at the older pond my friend suggested we just drive into the pond's edge so that we would not have to lift the water so high to fill the barrels.

We did, and slowly filled the barrels. When this was done, my friend decided to make the mules swim by driving them into deep water.

A couple of lunges by these kind and innocent brutes brought us to deep water! In fact it was so deep that the wagon went under water causing the barrels to float away. In the meantime the mules flopped up and down desperately, just barely able to hold their noses above the water. They couldn't escape. Only one thing could save them and avert disaster. I needed to quickly go into the muddy water and unhook the team from the wagon.

I immediately dove into the water and struggled blindly to find the one bolt on the wagon tongue that would release the poor critters. Upon finding the bolt and lifting it out the mules popped to the surface of the pond like corks!

Now the quandary we were in was how to get the wagon out. I ran to the farm shop and found a log-chain and managed to get it hooked to the rear of the wagon.

The mules were so spooked they wanted nothing to do with the water, however we finally got them hooked to the rear of the wagon and hauled it to the bank.

The old steel wagons were not supposed to be rolled backwards that far and one of the nuts holding a rear wheel came off about the time we reached the bank of the pond. Getting the wheel back on and retrieving the barrels, some of which had sunk in the pond, and refilling them before Grandpa discovered what had happened was our next task.

All of this was accomplished in record time.

Needless to say we earned our degrees in common sense that hot, summer day. We never tried to make the mules swim again.

Later, the Robinson Farm would be home to country singer Alan Jackson. Many times I have driven by the old pond with the fabulous mansion nearby and wondered if he would enjoy that story.

My First Night In The U.S. Army

As I approached my twenty-third birthday in 1961 another major change was approaching. I had been classified as 1-A by the local Selective Service Draft Board. My status had been revised by the board and along with other local men I was selected to enter the Army on December 12, 1961.

The night before I entered the Army, I had my going-away and birthday party all rolled into one.

I was sad to leave Carolyn and enter the Army. Her father, a preacher and a home-builder, had built us our first home at 1111 Parkview Drive in Franklin. We were all set for the joys of marriage and life together. Then that special letter from Uncle Sam arrived in the mail. "Greetings! We want you for military service!"

In order to fulfill my patriotic duty I reported to the local draft board office on Fourth Avenue South in Franklin at the specified time. Our group was loaded onto a Franklin Interurban bus and transported to the induction center on White Bridge Road in Nashville. After an

initial orientation and a cursory physical exam we were
sworn into the service of our country. From the
induction center we were taken to Union Station where
later that evening we boarded a train to Memphis. In
Memphis we boarded a double-decker Greyhound bus
for transport to Fort Chaffee, Arkansas.

The future soldiers I was traveling with were headed by a
young man who was re-enlisting into the service. The
soldier gave us wise instructions about how to survive
the next two years.

"If you have any money in your pockets you should
place it in your jockey shorts when you go to bed
tonight," he said, offering his first advice. "If you do not,
someone will steal it."

Later that night as bedtime approached I followed his
advice. When I awoke the next morning my first reaction
was to reach for my billfold. It was missing! I found it
about four bunks down with my twenty bucks still
inside.

My life prior to induction into the military had been
centered on church and religion. From childhood my
loving grandmother had taught me right from wrong and
to live a peaceful life. I married my childhood
sweetheart. She was the daughter of a preacher who had
a profound influence on me. I was conscientiously
opposed to killing, so I had registered with the draft
board as a conscientious objector. I had given careful
thought to this decision after consulting with my father-
in-law and other ministers of the church I attended.

I had been told by one of the ministers that I would be scorned, black-listed, and given rough treatment because of my status as a conscientious objector. He had suffered severely for having the same status during the Second World War.

Well I was a big boy – I could take it.

I thought my trial had begun the first morning of my service, when a huge sergeant burst through the barracks door and screamed at the top of his lungs.

"I want all the blank! blank! blank! conscientious objectors to fall out right now!"

I did not move. I was frightened beyond words.

In the next instant a frail-looking young soldier down the barracks row slowly made his way to the front of the room. Pvt. Charles Hill of Hattiesburg, Mississippi was reporting to this giant who was probably going to eat him alive.

He looked so alone and in order to assist him I slowly stepped forward to meet whatever the future held.

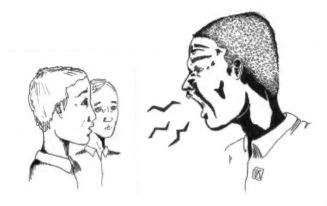

As we approached this giant of a sergeant exclaimed in a booming voice, "You two soldiers are the luckiest men in the world! You are headed to Fort Sam Houston, Texas!"

Later that day I made my first airplane flight on a DC-3 military transport to San Antonio. There at Fort Sam Houston I learned that the Army had established a special training detachment to train conscientious

objectors as combat medics. I also learned during my
training that this classification of combat medic was one
of the most dangerous jobs a soldier could find himself
doing during combat.

I immediately started looking for a safer place to hide for
the next two years!

I had two years of typing under teacher Sara Jordan at
Franklin High School my junior and senior years. So I
was a good typist by the time I got to the Army. Because
of my skills as a typist and clerk I was eventually assigned
the cushy job of secretary and driver to the lieutenant
colonel who commanded my permanent duty station in
the 54th Field Hospital at Fort Carson, Colorado.

Fort Carson is located near Colorado Springs, on the
slope of the Rocky Mountains. Carolyn and I had a
wonderful new experience there, exploring the nearby
ghost towns of the Rockies as well as Pike's Peak and
surrounding areas during our stay.

Life Is Just A Shadow

It was springtime in 1957 in Franklin, Tennessee. May of that year was to be one of the most beautiful months of my life.

I was to graduate from high school, a culmination of many years of study and part-time attendance in school. Finally I would be finished with my schooling but only beginning my education. Growing up on a farm had required me to miss many school days during harvest time. However by swapping phone calls with a friend and neighbor who was a fellow student, I managed to accumulate enough points to pass all of my subjects.

The graduation exercises were held at the old Franklin High School gymnasium. Fire had destroyed the beautiful old school a year or so before and the new high school had not yet been completed.

All during high school and early childhood I had been in love with my childhood sweetheart. We had courted with such devotion that we knew we would marry and spend the rest of our lives together. Well things took a backward turn about the beginning of my senior year. My sweetheart fell for another young man who came courting with a much better car and money to spend. I was devastated! Life was over! No chance that our long courtship would ever be revived!

The day after graduation found me riding a Greyhound to El Dorado, Arkansas. There I would rekindle a friendship with a sweet little red-headed miss that I had known from revival meetings that her preacher-father held at our church. Sue would help me heal and time would make me forget my old sweetheart.

It just did not happen that way! All the hours spent with Sue were hours talking about her old boyfriend and my old girlfriend. We spent many happy hours together but nothing could turn our hearts from our former loves.

One night as I lay sleeping in the one room that I rented in a large boarding house, I was awakened by an intense yearning. My heart was forever stricken with the beautiful girl that I had left behind. In my distress I turned to the window and looked upward where millions of stars were dancing in the night sky.

My mind was drawn back to a long row of lilacs that bordered our garden as I grew up. I could smell the wonderful fragrance of those flowers as I lay in distress. My mind dwelled upon the biblical character Job, who said, "Man born of woman is but a few days and full of trouble."

I thought, Job, you were so right.

I reached over to the night table and turned on a small tape recorder that I had placed there and the words that follow in this song came straight from above.

"Life Is A Shadow" has been performed in many church services and a number of funerals for the past many years. However the most important performance came not from me but from my granddaughter, Jesse Vieira da Rocha, who sings it with a marvelous voice that must be inspired by God who was the creator of the song.

"Life Is A Shadow"

Did you ever hear an echo in the silence of the night?
Or watch a little birdie make its first small flight.
Did you ever stand in wonder and as your wonder grew,
Know that God in Heaven was watching over you?

There is life in a tree so tall, life in a birdie small,
Life is just a shadow, and shadows pass away.
Life in the birds that sing, God gives life to everything,
Life is just a shadow, and shadows pass away.

Did you ever smell the fragrance of the lilacs in the
spring?
Or wade the brook in summer, and hear God's creatures
sing?
I have my friend that's how I know life is a gift of God,
I thank Him for this life I live and for this path I trod.

There is life in a tree so tall, life in a birdie small,
Life is just a shadow, and shadows pass away.
Life in the birds that sing, God gives life to everything.
Life is just a shadow, and shadows pass away.

How I Became The Star For Just One Game

The winter of 1953 found me finishing the eighth grade at Lipscomb Elementary School. The school is in northern Williamson County on Concord Road and at the time had eight grades and about 130 students.

There were about twelve students in the eighth grade including me. Our teacher and school principal was Mr. A.B. Thomas. He was also the baseball and basketball coach.

The basketball court was a dirt spot that had been graded to a somewhat level condition at the foot of a hill. There were six or seven boys on the team. Most of the team members were farm boys who spent more time plowing behind mules and milking cows than they spent practicing basketball.

Grassland School was also a member of the grade-school basketball league. The challenge came from Grassland's principal to Mr. Thomas for a basketball game.

The game could not be played outside at either school due to bad weather so it was moved to the Franklin High

64

School gym. This large gym was more like a hole in the ground with a balcony high above the floor where onlookers could observe the action below.

Our team made a valiant effort and the score was tied with about two minutes left in the game. I was probably the worst player on the team and had not played the entire game. Coach Thomas must have felt sorry for me because with the final score still very much in question he called my name and sent me into the action.

Well what do you know? The confusion that I encountered upon entering the game was most troubling. Which goal was our team's goal? What if I really got my hands on the ball?

Suddenly the basketball caromed off the backboard of the Grassland team and landed smack in my hands. In desperation I flung the ball back at the wrong goal!

The best player on the Grassland team became totally confused as he rebounded the ball. In a mad rush he dribbled the ball to the other end of the floor and sank a basket on the Lipscomb side! He became the goat and I became the hero.

Of course everyone knew that my action was all planned and on-purpose (sure!).

The final score was 17 - 15 in favor of the Lipscomb team.

It was nice to ride back to school with all the other team members recognizing me as their hero.

'Daddy I'm Coming Home'

"Daddy, I'm coming home."

These were welcome words to the ears of anxious parents from a young daughter and fourth-year college student.

For some time this sweet child had been involved with a man everyone knew would be a terrible life partner.

What to do? When the parents' advice failed they turned it over to Jesus. He would hear their petition and answer just in time.

When the call came, "Daddy, I'm coming home," there was instant relief that the parents' prayers had been answered. Four long years of time and college expenses were forgotten. Everything was going to be just fine.

The reply was simple.

"Honey, I'll be up to get you in the morning," said the father to his little girl.

The next day was a whirlwind of activity as the rental truck was secured and headed in the direction of a child in distress. Nothing else mattered except to arrive before a change of mind and heart could be made. The trip home was not a joyous occasion as sorrow filled the cab of the rental truck. All the reassurance in the world could not assure this child that God was intervening in her life.

But God did intervene! Shortly after coming home this sweet child took a job waiting tables at a local restaurant. This would be temporary work until future life decisions could be made. One night while she was working late at the restaurant a fine and eligible man appeared.

This wonderful gentleman was seeking a date. From the moment he saw this pretty girl he was smitten for life.

Now more than twenty-five years later, two proud parents are thankful to God for a wonderful son-in-law and two beautiful grandchildren.

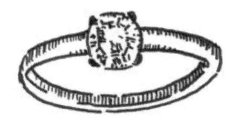

I Smell Frying Chicken (So It Must Be Sunday Morning)

Many of the memories of my childhood have faded. They have been washed away by the calendar and the years that have come and gone.

However, one of those memories will never fade: the memory of Sunday morning. It was a special time on our farm. Sunday morning usually meant thirty minutes of extra sleep and fried chicken for breakfast.

My usual wake-up time during the week was about five o'clock in the morning. This early rising gave me ample time for morning chores. Before walking the mile or so to the school bus it was my duty to go to the barn and feed our stock, milk four or five cows by hand, and return to the house for breakfast.

This was a typical farm boy's life during the fifties in the Mallory Valley area of Williamson County.

I can still smell that chicken frying in a hot pan on those

Sunday mornings! The tantalizing smell wafted all around the yard and even drifted into the barn where I was busy milking and feeding our cows.

The chicken frying took a bit of special preparation by my grandmother. You see, there were no chicken factories in Franklin in those days. We usually had a large flock of chickens roaming the yard. They roosted at night in low tree branches or in the makeshift henhouse located nearby. It was easy for Grandma to slip into the henhouse early on Sunday mornings and catch a nice, frying-sized chicken or old hen before they were aroused for the day.

The axe lay nearby on the woodpile chopping-block and Grandma was an expert at slaughtering. She had gained these skills from a lifetime of experience. The boiling pot of water was ready for dousing the freshly killed chicken, and feathers were efficiently removed. In the meantime the old iron skillet was heating up on the wood-burning stove in the kitchen ready to receive this fresh chicken.

Oh, the smell! I remember my rush to finish my chores before breakfast was placed on the kitchen table. If I arrived too late the only chicken left for me would be the north end of a south-flying chicken. I really preferred a drumstick!

How About A Quart Of Compression?

In late 1957 the Ford Motor Company brought forth its dream-car. The Edsel automobile was to be the savior of the company in competing with General Motors in the production of American cars.

The Edsel became a total failure for the company and after three model years it was abandoned by Ford. The reasons for its failure are many and that is a subject for a future story.

This tale is about me, a young country boy who was given the job of parts manager for the Edsel dealer in Nashville. I had applied for a job with Mr. Charlie Morton, owner of Morton Edsel Sales located at 1500 Broadway. Mr. Morton fired his parts manager who was being paid 125 dollars per week and hired me to take over for the lowly sum of forty dollars per week.

A few weeks after assuming the job of managing the parts department I became the object of a little fun from the service manager and some of the shop employees. Mr. Harold Jackson, the shop foreman, approached the parts counter and asked for a quart of compression. Well we all know (now) there is no such thing as compression sold in cans. Compression is what the engine needs to function properly and it is not something that can be sold in a can. How was I to know that I was being set up for a fun trip by the whole dealership?

I knew that if compression was something I was supposed to have in my parts department, I was fresh out. I told Mr. Jackson I was out of compression but I would try to get him some from a neighboring car dealer or parts store. There were a number of car dealers nearby and I immediately started my search.

First the parts store next door – where they were also out. Mr. Jackson had called them and let them in on the joke. He also told them to send me to Ralph Nichols Cadillac across Broadway.

After calling and visiting several stores to find them all "out of compression in a can" I realized that I had been had. With much chagrin and with my head down I returned to the parts department and hid under the counter until quitting time.

I will always remember that compression does not come in a can. I also learned there were some things I did not know about the Edsel or automobiles in general.

My Brief Career As A Barber

It was a typical night in the Army barracks at Fort Sam Houston, Texas, in late December 1961. The sergeant in charge of these seventy or so raw recruits had left the area.

Before leaving he had informed the group that there would be an "in-rank inspection" tomorrow morning. Our entire squad was mystified as to what this could mean. Putting our heads together we realized that we would be given a fine-tooth-comb going-over and everything had better be ship-shape and according to Army regulations.

This inspection would mean that boots had to be spit-shined; brass had to be polished; and uniforms had to be clean and starched. Long hair was hated by the military brass. You may have just had a haircut three days ago but your hair could still be considered too long.

The Post Barber Shop had long since closed and a few of the troops were anxious about their hair being too long. The inspecting officer could give them a "gig" for this infraction. A gig was a bad thing. If you accumulated too many gigs, you could be denied a pass for the weekend.

Since I had been appointed temporary sergeant and was in charge at the time it was up to me to appease the group.

"Does anyone have a pair of clippers?" I asked. "I was a barber in civilian life and I would be glad to cut your hair."

Unfortunately for one poor soldier a pair of clippers was promptly brought out.

It was strictly against Army rules to cut hair in the barracks. We had no regard for these silly rules! We quickly set up a foot-locker for a stool and a towel for protection from the residue of hair that was about to start falling.

Pvt. Arter Gary of Louisville, Kentucky quickly draped the towel around his shoulders and proudly became the first victim. The line for service stretched almost to the rear of the barracks.

Well, the more I cut the more soldiers fell out of line. Poor Pvt. Gary kept feeling of his head and asking, addressing me by nick-name, "How are you doing, Andy?"

"Things are going well and I will soon be finished," I replied.

I thought cutting hair would be a very simple thing. It was not. I just could not seem to get the clippers steady as I proceeded through Pvt. Gary's hair. There were gaps to the skin in many places.

Soon the line was empty. No other soldier wanted to be butchered like this!

All at once Pvt. Gary flung off the towel and exclaimed, "Andy, you jackass, you have ruined me!"

Rushing to the latrine he inspected himself in the mirror and came back in a fighting mood.

Fortunately for me, sanity prevailed and I paid for him to visit a real barber the next morning before that dreaded "in-rank inspection" took place.

Making An Appointment For My Competitor; Or, Payback For Dirty Tricks Played On Me

The hardships and joys of direct-selling are well known to me. I learned my trade from some of the top trainers in the business. The tricks taught to me by them and some developed by trial and error served me well in the time that I sold cookware to young single working girls in the Middle Tennessee area.

I had entered the direct-selling field by necessity in early 1967. I was employed by the Ford Motor Company glass manufacturing plant in West Nashville. Carolyn was working as a secretary at Baptist Hospital. When she became pregnant with our second child it was necessary for her to leave her employment. I began to search for part-time work to supplement our income until she could have the baby and return to work.

My need was just fifty-five dollars a week!

In my search I answered a blind ad in the Nashville

newspaper. The help-wanted ad read simply, "Fifty-Five Dollars A Week" for three evenings a week and Saturday. I quickly called the number listed and the phone call was answered by a gentleman who would not tell me a thing about the position. He would only say that he was setting up appointments for an interview. I took the bait.

Upon arrival at the appointed place and time a few nights later I noticed a brand-new Pontiac Grand Prix outside the door. As I entered the small room a gentleman wearing a hundred-dollar suit of clothes introduced himself as Vestal Harding. He told me that he would be conducting the interview a little later.

As other applicants came into the room I strolled around and saw a small projector in place. The title of the record in place was *Wearever.* My mind connected – cookware!

I thought, Oh my, this is a job selling cookware! I wanted to leave but the interview was about to begin.

I was seated among a number of other hungry-looking young men seeking employment. I stayed as Mr. Harding showed the film and took his position at a small black-board in the front of the room. He explained how we were to be paid these fifty-five dollars.

"Show this product to ten single working girls a week and you will make three sales," he told us. "Your commission on these sales will exceed the promised fifty-five dollars per week."

He went on to tell us all the glories of this product and how easy it was to sell.

No one stayed for the one-on-one interview except me! I only stayed to challenge him as a fraud.

"You lied!" I exclaimed as he started his next phase – recruiting.

It was early in the evening and time for ending the recruiting session when he offered his next hook.

"How would you like to see me make a hundred dollars tonight?" he asked.

"Well," I replied, "are we going to rob a store? All the banks are closed!"

"No," said Mr. Harding, "we are going to sell some cookware."

And sell he did! He made two calls in West Nashville and had two orders. I felt like he had planted those two girls in order to impress me. However he had their checks in his hand as proof. Also these young ladies had given him more names to call on the next night.

It was late when we returned to his office and I tried to comprehend all that I had seen and heard that night. I learned that the Wearever Cookware Company was the original waterless cookware. It was marketed as a way of conserving all the rich vitamins and minerals by cooking foods without adding water. The precious vitamins and minerals that might otherwise be poured down the sink, would be saved for the family's consumption.

I could hardly wait to get started. When I arrived home that first night I told my wife I had purchased a set of samples and she was mortified!

"Honey," she said, "you are not a salesman."

She did not know, but I had learned, that salesmen are not born but are trained. I was receiving my training from the expert Mr. Harding.

Finally, after two or three nights of intensive training I reported the next afternoon for final instructions and to pick up my new set of gleaming cookware samples. I had been trained never to call on a girl without a job. But my first call was just that – on a girl with no job, and still in high school. Although I sold her and her mother on the cookware she could not buy because she had no job. Problem solved: Just call on girls who were working!

My next stop was a sweet little lady named Ann Brown, who lived not more than a mile from my house. I sold her a wonderful new method of cooking and she gave me a check, and a friend's name. My next stop was a mile away, at the home of Ann Talent. My expert salesmanship produced another sale!

My income on two sales: $47.60 and $37.10. The checks were in my hand. I moved as fast as possible to the local market and cashed those checks. That was $84.70, for my evening's work.

"Small bills, sir," I told the clerk.

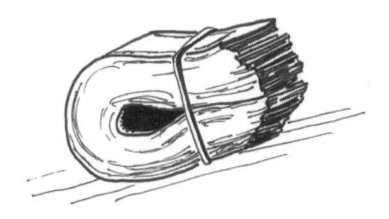

Hurrying home to a pregnant wife who was already asleep, I hastened to our bedroom and turned on the overhead light. I cast the small bills like confetti into the air and watched her scramble!

"Where did you get all this money?" she asked.

"It was easy," I said, telling her about my night.
"Tomorrow night I am going back for more!"

Many long nights followed – some producing great sales
and some adding up to zero. Three years passed, door
after door after door, and story after story. I came to
believe in myself as a salesman.

Unfortunately there were some unscrupulous people
involved in direct sales. I learned of one of them and his
dirty tricks one night as I arrived at a customer's home to
find out why she had not picked up her order at the local
post office.

It seems that this competitor had arrived at her house
and learned of her purchase of Wearever. He smooth-
talked her into buying his product and leaving the
Wearever to return to the factory. This was a costly thing
for me as part of my commission was held until the
order was accepted. My scheme was born that instant: I
would break this outlaw in our business from sucking
eggs!

I returned to my office and called this salesman,
pretending to be a local dentist.

"Sir," I said, "I understand that you sell a good brand of
waterless cookware."

"Of course!" he replied. "I sell the very best! Yes, sir!"

"Well," I said, "my wife has a birthday coming up in
about a month and I would like to buy her a new set of

cookware. I do not want her to know about this. Would you come by my office for a demonstration?"

The appointment was made for the following morning.

"I'll be at your office at eight," he agreed.

"That will give us time before my appointments begin," I said.

"Do not pay any attention to my sweet receptionist," I told him. "She will try to keep you from seeing me knowing I am so busy. But just push on around her and come back to my office."

I made it to the area early and purchased a cup of coffee at a nearby restaurant. Here I could easily see the action as it took place.

Mr. Low-Dealing Salesman was very prompt – arriving at exactly eight o'clock.

As he exited his shiny car he straightened his necktie and reached for his sample set in the rear seat. As he walked briskly and erect to the front door of the dentist's office I could only imagine what was about to take place.

It did not take long for a disheveled- and harried-looking Low-Dealing Salesman to exit the dentist's office. His tie was crooked and his hat was falling off; his sample kit was half-packed with panhandles protruding from its sides.

I finished my coffee and headed for my office. I gave the Low-Dealing Salesman time to get to his office and rang him up.

"Well," I asked, "how did the appointment go?"

"So you set me up!" he said with curses not printable.

"Yes, and if you ever send another set of my cookware back to the factory I am going to set up appointments from the Smoky Mountains to the Mississippi River," I told him.

"The only way you will ever know if they are real is to check them out just as you did the good doctor!"

I never had another set of Wearever returned!

'Give 'Em Hell Harry' – 'The Buck Stops Here'

Harry S. Truman came to Washington, D.C. in 1934 as an elected senator from Missouri. He left Washington in early 1953 after serving as vice president under Franklin Delano Roosevelt and as president of the United States upon Mr. Roosevelt's death in 1945. President Truman had a plaque on his desk that read, "The Buck Stops Here."

Leaving the White House in early 1953 President Truman and his wife Bess packed their belongings into his personal car and drove home to Missouri.

Seemingly insurmountable odds faced Mr. Truman in the presidential campaign of 1948.

As a ten-year-old boy I was living in a sharecropper shack with my grandparents a mile east of the Franklin Public Square. My grandfather was a Roosevelt- and Truman-Democrat. Grandpa and I listened to the election returns on an old battery-powered radio. About midnight it was announced that Gov. Thomas E. Dewey of New York had won the election!

Grandpa was totally distressed. Before retiring to bed that night he told me, "Well, son, we had better get ready for four hard years!"

I did not understand how things could get much harder. We were already living on salted pork belly, white beans and cornbread with a fried wild rabbit once in a while.

HARRY S. TRUMAN

Well sure enough, joy came in the morning! The radio revealed that Harry S. Truman had come through and would continue to be our president for the next four years. I cannot remember if things got any better for this poor farm family.

There is one thing I do know: If we could have a Harry Truman running for president today I would change my allegiance to his party.

At seventy-six years old, I sure hope to live long enough to have that privilege.

Hills Of My Heart

In the winter of 1951 I moved with my grandparents to the historic Walters Farm located on Mallory Road just east of where the CoolSprings Galleria is today. Of course there was no interstate highway and Mallory Lane was a one-lane gravel road. The old Mallory schoolhouse was still standing at the corner of Mallory Lane and Mallory Road although it was vacant due to the consolidation of Williamson County schools.

The Walters Farm was fertile ground for farming and observing the natural world. Grandpa and I along with other members of the family tended to the many acres with mule teams. Our home was a large pre-Civil War residence with the typical double front porches and many chimneys.

The farm afforded many opportunities for exploring. My favorite pastime was riding my pony Molly on the high hills on the eastern boundary of the farm. These hills were the high point in the area and miles of the surrounding farmland could be seen from this focal point.

The most interesting sight found during my exploring was a large field of daffodils among the briers and brambles that covered the hillsides. For many years I wondered how row upon row of spring flowers could have been planted there. Thousands of daffodils of many varieties came up every spring and the more I visited the area the more of a mystery it became to me: When were they planted, and by whom?

Fast-forward to about 1973. I was engaged as a real estate broker and had an office in Franklin. One day a middle-aged man came to my office seeking employment. He introduced himself as Joe Walters.

I was immediately taken back in my memory to the daffodil fields on the Walters Farm and without hesitation I asked if he might have known Mr. Billy Ed Walters.

He replied, "Gosh, mister, how could you have possibly known Billy Ed Walters? He was my father!"

I explained that I had spent some of the most wonderful days of my childhood on the Walters Farm and I had to have an answer to the mystery of the daffodils that were blooming on the hillsides.

It was spring in Franklin and the daffodils were in full bloom. Joe Walters accompanied me to the daffodil fields. We drove as far as possible, then made our way through the briers and bushes and there they were.

"Why?" I asked him, and listened intently as he told the story.

"In the early years of the Great Depression my family needed a cash crop that could be harvested in the spring," he explained. "My father planted the daffodils as a means of supporting his family."

Joe Walters recalled arriving home from school with his brothers and sisters in the evenings, and going to the

daffodil fields to pick and gather them into bundles.
These bundles were then taken to street vendors in
Nashville on some days and further south to
Chattanooga on other days. The bundles were sold to
street vendors for five cents per bundle.

Joe worked with me selling real estate for a number of
years prior to his retirement and we had a good time
swapping memories.

"The Daffodil Field"

I want to go back to the hills of my heart
Where daffodils wave in the wind.
To see a small part of my vanishing youth
And be a small boy once again.

Millions and millions of daffodils there
Planted by small hands unknown.
They come every year like soldiers in rank –
God's beautiful seasons are sown.

My heart wants a chance to rest for a spell
Away from my work-a-day world;
Far back in the hills where I played as a child;
Where nature's grand beauty unfurls.

So thank you friend for sharing with me
A moment or two from my past.
We're making a memory that never shall die;
And our friendship forever will last.

Someday when I'm weary beyond all my strength;
And the time has come to lie down;
Please plant me there in the daffodil field
Until the last trumpet shall sound.

The Joy Of Fatherhood; Or, How My First Son Became Known As Victor

Many are the joys of being a father and I could not have been more pleased when the word came to me in October, 1962 that our first child had been born.

I was serving in the Army and our field hospital was out on the plains of Colorado several miles south of our home-base at Fort Carson. Some months after my arrival at Fort Carson the 54th Field Hospital was deactivated, and we were training for assignment as the 67th Evacuation Hospital for a tour of duty in Vietnam.

The evacuation hospital would be the last treatment center for the wounded soldiers before they were evacuated to station hospitals in the United States or Germany.

Fortunately for me, I was discharged from service before my company was sent to Vietnam.

That fall day by chance I happened to be substituting at

the field telephone switchboard. As I attended the switchboard a call came from the American Red Cross asking to speak to the company commander. I plugged the cord into the colonel's slot and rang his phone. I listened intently as he answered and the Red Cross informed him that Pvt. Andrews's wife had gone to the hospital. Not stating the reason for her call she told the colonel that if it was at all possible Frank should come home to Tennessee.

The colonel did not know that Carolyn was expecting our first child. However he sent his orderly over and I was told to report to the headquarters tent immediately.

As I entered the headquarters tent the colonel met me with anguish in his face.

"Pvt. Andrews," he began, "I have just had a call from the Red Cross and you are to leave immediately and go home to Tennessee.

"It seems that your wife has suffered some ailment and is in need of you."

"Well," I replied, "I guess our baby has been born!"

Profanity then began bubbling from the colonel's mouth.

He exclaimed, "Hell, you could have told me that your wife was pregnant! Get your grip together and we'll have the orderly take you back to the barracks and you may leave to go home."

As soon as I reached the Army base I called home. We had been expecting a girl and had a sweet name picked for her. Well it was a boy and we had no name.

"What shall we name our son?" asked Carolyn.

As I was concentrating on our dilemma all the good times we had exploring the little ghost mining towns in the mountains west of Colorado Springs came to my mind. Victor was my favorite among these little ghost towns.

I replied, "Why don't we just name our son Victor?"

"That will be swell!" she agreed.

The next morning I managed to catch a military transport bound for Maxwell Air Force Base in Alabama. This was a major-general's plane transporting him and his staff on an inspection trip. Service was first class and the flight went fine.

As I was leaving the airport in a taxi bound for the bus station in Montgomery we crossed U.S. Highway 231. I asked the driver to stop. Franklin was about 250 miles due north. I would flag a ride home.

My first ride carried me all the way to Lewisburg, Tennessee. I was about thirty miles from home. I had walked in the dark about a mile when a group of high-school kids offered me a ride. It seems that they were headed for Columbia but would be glad to go out of their way and deliver me to my wife and son in Franklin.

It was a happy reunion with Carolyn and our first son, Victor.

I have told Victor many times how lucky he is.

"Son, you know Cripple Creek is just a few miles from Victor and that could have been my favorite ghost town," I kid him.

I am really glad I did not name my first son "Cripple Creek."

Since those long-ago Army days Victor has grown to manhood in a wonderful way. He has a sweet wife and four children Carolyn and I love dearly.

Victor's business acumen is well-known in our community. He has served as president of our family appraisal service since its beginning. Also, he is highly respected and his advice is often sought in business and political matters in the area.

The Night I Found Out I Needed Glasses

The spring of 1975 saw minor league baseball return to Nashville after an absence of many years. This return was due to the efforts of Mr. Larry Schmittou.

Larry had become my friend when we both worked at the Ford glass plant. Larry was working to pay for his education at Peabody College while I was working to support a wife and two children. Baseball was in Larry's blood as he had coached the Post 5 American Legion baseball team for several years. Later he gained further baseball experience as coach of the Vanderbilt University team.

Many times while we worked together on the night shift making glass for Ford cars, I worked two jobs so Larry could steal a two- or three-hour nap in order to return to his activities the next day. The other workers in the department helped by devising signals to use if the foreman was seen approaching.

Sleeping on the job was one of the few reasons to be fired as the union could not protect you in the event you were caught.

Most nights Larry was awakened by my singing "The Star-Spangled Banner."

Larry, who is presently involved in the bowling alley business, was an excellent promoter and when time came for organizing the return of baseball to Nashville he was a natural for the job. As one of his promotions Larry had the famous baseball players Ernie Banks and Phil Niekro attend one of his meetings. I felt highly honored to be invited to that particular meeting.

The Nashville Sounds became a successful baseball team due to Larry's promotion and management. Always playing near the top of the league they produced many future major league stars and had top attendance for several years.

One night Larry invited me to sing the national anthem before the game.

This was a highly promoted game with approximately ten thousand fans in attendance. Fans filled the seats at Herschel Greer Stadium and many lined the outfield along first and third bases.

I had sung the national anthem at many events including local horse shows and little league gatherings, but this was my elevation to the big leagues. I had just turned thirty-nine and as you know eyesight begins to fade a little at this age. So I prepared by writing the words down on a business card just in case they were needed.

Well they were most needed!

As I neared mid-way through the national anthem someone in the crowd behind home plate where I was stationed yelled, "Go ahead big Frank!"

I was stunned, but not yet lost. I had the words – it was
O.K.

But as I turned the card over in my hand and got the
words in focus I realized the words were upside-down.
What a dilemma! I stopped the national anthem in front
of the entire stadium and sang it again. That ended my
debut as a singer and permanently etched my name in
the Nashville Sounds history book as the man who
double-sang the national anthem.

By my finish that night the entire stadium was laughing
at me and my poor family listening at home was crying!

I am still looking for the raucous fan who did the yelling.
And if there had been a hole at home plate I would have
crawled in and would never have come out.

My Early Exit From Uncle Sam's Army; Or, How The Major Let Me Out Scot-Free!

I was honorably discharged from active military service on December 8, 1963. I had served two years of active service.

It had been an enjoyable experience in many ways. I had grown to love the beautiful state of Colorado and the city of Colorado Springs where I had performed my permanent duty. Uncle Sam in the early sixties required each soldier who was drafted into the military to serve two years of active duty, two years of active reserves and two years of inactive reserves. The active reserve duty required a soldier to report to an Army Reserve unit close to home for one weekend a month. A summer camp consisting of two weeks of active service was also required during the active reserve phase.

I was assigned to a P.O.W. Camp (inactive) in East Nashville. In time of war this prisoner of war detachment was responsible for the care and imprisonment of any captured enemy soldiers. The company was commanded by a major who was also performing his obligation for active reserve training. I became his company clerk. My duties as company clerk included typing orders and retiring them to the Department of the Army as soldiers fulfilled their obligations for active reserve duty.

Well enough of this playing Army! I was busy with my life. I had served my time! I had a real job now and was too busy to let the Army interfere.

My exit scheme worked as follows:

One Sunday morning I was in the process of preparing a number of records for shipment to the Army holding center. Wow! Like a bolt of lightning the idea hit me! Why not ship my records along with all the others I was sending out, and never show up again?

I carefully filled out all the necessary forms for all the sets of records that were being shipped that day. I placed my records in the middle. To carry out my scheme I carefully placed each set of records before the major for his signature. By this time I had earned his complete trust and he rarely looked at anything I presented for him to sign.

Later that day I followed normal procedure for shipping the records. I never returned to the P.O.W. camp. Also, I never heard anything else from the military. I later learned that there had been a fire in a St. Louis records warehouse where thousands of military records were stored. I have always hoped that my records were among the charred.

Over the next several months I spent some anxious days looking over my shoulder for a military policeman. He never came for me. It has now been over fifty years since that slight altering of the rules and records took place. I am beginning to think I may be home-free! Anyway at my age a stint in the Army could make me proud to say, "Freedom ain't free!"

Where Did All Of Those Horses Come From?

Though my time living in South Nashville was brief, and I soon returned to the farm, I gathered many stories there. The small apartment I shared with my sister, my mother and mother's new husband was located at 623 Second Avenue South. The neighborhood was mostly middle-class workers who commuted to area jobs by walking or by the city bus.

My mother was a waitress at the Hi Ho Restaurant near Vanderbilt Hospital. She worked a split shift. Her employment required her to arrive at work at 10 a.m. and work until 2 p.m. She then left work and reversed her bus travel home just to repeat the same process when she returned to work for her 4 p.m. to 10 p.m. shift.

Our neighborhood at the time encompassed several city blocks including the Children's Museum and Howard School. Most important, though, it also included the Capitol Theatre near Lafayette Street.

Neighborhood children played in the street and neighboring yards as well as on the school grounds. I made friends with a pretty girl down the street whose family name was Crocker. I do not remember the first name of this pretty girl; however I do remember going to her house one night to watch a new-fangled thing that was called a television. I was eleven years old.

As I approached the Crocker home that night I remember well that the whole house was dark. Slipping quietly into the hallway I heard noises that sounded like running horses. I turned to the living room and opened the door and to my surprise across the room I saw the horses on a small, odd-looking contraption that was similar to a radio, but had an eye in the front that was all lit up.

That eye had horses and cowboys flashing into the darkened room where several people were seated. I could not believe my eyes!

My first reaction was to move around to the back of the television to find out how the cowboys with their horses had gotten into this small box. After feeling all around I knew that this must be magic and I was in a brand-new world.

Television in its infancy had come to Nashville! It was only broadcast a few hours a day. I spent many happy hours at the Crocker home that summer as they had the only television in our neighborhood.

And oh yes! That first television program was *Hopalong Cassidy* and I became an immediate fan.

A Close Call In Downtown Franklin

The old concrete silos on First Avenue in downtown Franklin are stark reminders of a time gone by. For many years farmers from miles around would bring their grain to Franklin for processing at the J.B. Lillie Flour Mill on the bank of the Harpeth River. Since 1869 when it was established by Joshua B. Lillie the mill has stood as a local landmark. Today the remaining silos stand silent witness to the old farm-centered economy.

I well remember as a small child sitting up late at night on the farm shelling corn that would be hauled to the mill the next day on a farm wagon pulled by a team of mules. There the corn would be traded for Lillie Mill flour. The flour would be packed in ten- and twenty-five-pound bags made from pretty, domestic material that later wound up as dresses for the farm girls.

January 8, 1958 found me working in downtown Franklin. This is the day the famous Lillie Mill was destroyed by fire. From my job at the Five Points Garage on Fifth Avenue North my coworkers and I heard the

112

sirens sounding the alarm.

Hurriedly we followed the sounds to the fire on First Avenue.

When I arrived the crowd had gathered along the opposite side of First Avenue and the mill was in complete surrender to the fire.

We all watched as the firemen worked helplessly to contain the blaze.

Out of the crowd of firemen and helpers came the fire chief. He was waving his hands in all directions and shouting at us.

"Get back, get back," warned the chief. "There are welding tanks in the building containing acetylene gas. They are likely to explode at any minute!"

No one paid much attention to him until all at once, "BOOM, BOOM," out of the fire and smoke came a canister of twisted metal and fire that flew over our heads and pierced the attic of a house behind where we were standing. The house was immediately engulfed in flames.

It only took a few seconds for the watching crowd to scatter to safer places!

I returned to work feeling lucky to have survived such a close call.

Oh, my! What if the canister had traveled just ten feet lower?

Baptism In The Cold, Cold Creek; Or, The Day I Gave My Heart To Jesus

There is a small concrete dam across the creek that is visible along the three hundred block of Sheffield Place in the Royal Oaks Subdivision in eastern Franklin. This small, four-foot-high dam was originally constructed to block the creek to supply water for livestock. In the mid-1940s it also served as a neighborhood swimming hole.

This is where I learned to swim along with many other members of the family. Our large family lived in two sharecropper shacks on the farm. The two shacks were separated by the small creek that crossed the farm.

Grandmother Sullivan, the matriarch of my family, raised her thirteen children along with my sister and me. This tiny woman who never weighed more than ninety-five pounds stood four feet, eleven inches tall and was fearless in her tasks.

She was also the family spiritual leader. She held prayer sessions at her feet every night and had scripture readings that still resonate in my memory today.

Grandma had accepted Jesus into her life at a very early age. Through all of her difficult life she held a close relationship with Jesus and she wanted all of her children and grandchildren to serve Jesus. He was her anchor in times of need, happiness or grief.

It was summertime and this meant revival time at our local church. The Gospel Lighthouse Pentecostal Church was established in the early 1940s by Walter Lee and Ovella Smithson. This wonderful pastor and his wife

116

later became a father- and mother-in-law to me when I married their oldest daughter Carolyn.

Our church building was located on Forrest Street in the Lynnhurst section of Franklin. The building was humble: a concrete-block structure where the Gospel of Jesus Christ was preached several times a week.

Our family would sometimes walk three or more miles to church along with other farm families who lived nearby.

On a Saturday morning one warm spring day I learned from Grandma that there was to be a baptism in our creek later that day.

"Grandma," I asked, "may I be baptized?"

She replied, "Son, if you have really repented of all of your sins and believe in Jesus it is time for you to be baptized."

Preparations were made for the crowd that would gather later that day. The Rev. Petty was visiting from a northern state and would do the baptizing. Other congregants would worship the Lord as the cold waters of the creek washed away the multitude of sins that had weighed so heavily upon all the converts.

I remember the water was extremely cold as the preacher took my hand and led me into the creek that afternoon. There was shouting on the banks as I gave my heart to Jesus. I have never been sorry for my conversion and baptism. Today almost seventy years later that same wonderful Jesus is still very present. He has had a lasting impact on my life.

In the same way that Grandma coached me in my early years I have tried to challenge my children and grandchildren to always put Jesus first. I am glad to see Jesus present in the lives of my children and grandchildren today.

Thank God for the cold, cleansing waters of that long-ago creek!

My Son The Newspaper Reporter

I have always had a thirst for the excitement of a newsroom – where information arrives, is weighed and refined, considered and published. The idea of all the important news from all around filtering into one little spot in the town has always fascinated me.

I had the opportunity to work for a newspaper in the summer of 1957. I had graduated from Franklin High School and, looking for love that would not come true, I made my way to El Dorado, Arkansas.

In my rooming-house quarters I had a bed, table and chair. A bath down the hall was shared with many others. My charge for this luxury room and one meal a day was eleven dollars per week.

After a diligent search for employment I found a job at the *News-Times* daily newspaper. My starting position was proof-boy. This duty called for me to bicycle all over El Dorado with copies of the advertisements the local merchants had purchased. The merchants were given the

119

chance to make corrections or changes to the ads before they were published. After the inspections the corrected advertisements were returned to the make-up room where the linotype operators could reset the type.

In those days newspapers were printed from lead letters of the alphabet put in place by sweaty men who toiled in unbelievable heat and noise. Most of the operators were older men who had spent their lifetimes under these conditions and they could be quite cranky at times.

I caught newspaper fever! Every police call was monitored and every weather report was closely watched. Reporters were dispatched to any fire or accident to gather information for the story that was needed to keep the paper competitive with other news outlets in the area.

I worked diligently that summer performing my duties. I was rewarded with an offer to begin training to become a newspaper reporter. Unfortunately for my newspaper reporting career, love called – from my old sweetheart back home. I just could not resist the urge to return home to the girl that I loved. My newspaper career died before it really started.

Then many years later along came my son Brent. After many years of reminiscing about the newspaper business I could now relive the joy through him. His editorship of a large college newspaper won him awards and recognition as a good writer and reporter. After college he was employed by a number of newspapers. His writing and reporting skills have been recognized by the

Tennessee Press Association.

Today Brent is employed in the family appraisal business. His writing skills developed as a front-line newspaper reporter are valuable assets as he describes properties and market conditions in his everyday work.

His writing and business interests are also reflected in his small publishing company. To date Chronic Discontent Books has published five books and a number of others are in the works.

Maybe the seed of desire to write good stories and see them in print was passed from father to son.

I trust that I will live to see the best seller that is brewing in Brent's mind.

Note On Illustrations

Dear Nanny and Poppy,

There are no words to really describe the blessings of your generosity to the family, the business and myself. There is not a doubt in my mind that you two would make sacrifices to everyone else until there was nothing left to give. It is an inspiration to see that you have gone through trials in life, yet continue to give so generously.

I will never be able to thank you enough for providing a means to pursue my dreams and goals. Because of your unwavering support, there is enough money to pay room and board and tuition fees, and I have an excellent and trustworthy truck to take me there. The only way I can think to repay you is to pass along those blessings when the time comes.

I love you extraordinarily! Also, I am sending prayers for Poppy's book! It will be a treasure for the city of Franklin and a beloved heirloom for the family. I truly enjoyed every minute of creating the drawings.

With Love, Hannah Andrews

About the Author

Frank Andrews settled into the real estate business in the 1970s as a real estate broker and appraiser. He recently achieved Realtor Emeritus status with the National Association of Realtors. He has been married to Carolyn for 58 years.

More information on the Internet at
http://chronicdiscontent.blogspot.com